THE LITTLE BOOK OF BARBECUE TIPS

AN

THE LITTLE BOOK OF BARBECUE TIPS

ANDREW LANGLEY

Absolute Press

First published in Great Britain in 2006 by
Absolute Press
Scarborough House, 29 James Street West
Bath BA1 2BT, England
Phone 44 (0) 1225 316013 **Fax** 44 (0) 1225 445836
E-mail info@absolutepress.co.uk
Web www.absolutepress.co.uk

Reprinted 2009

A catalogue record of this book is available from the British Library

ISBN 9781904573371

Printed and bound in China by Hung Hing

'Come on baby, light my fire'

Robbie Krieger / Jim Morrison

1

Buy the right barbecue for your needs.

If you want quick results – burgers and steaks seared over high heat – then go for a simple open-top grill. If you want to cook things more slowly – whole chickens and ribs of beef – buy a kettle grill. This has a lid which cuts down the air intake and gives a steadier, lower level of heat.

2

Suit the grill to the size of the site.
For safety and social reasons,

make sure there's plenty of space around the barbecue.

On a balcony or small patio, use a compact, portable grill which can be swiftly packed away, or the handy cast-iron hibachi developed in Japan.

3

Build your own barbie.

Anyone with a modicum of bricklaying skills can construct a barbecue to their own preferred pattern and size.

But beware:

ordinary bricks and breeze blocks can contain air pockets which cause nasty explosions when fiercely heated. Use special fire bricks instead.

4

The simplest barbecue of all

can be made

in a few minutes.

Strip the turf from a 2 metre square patch of lawn. Lay two double rows of bricks about 30cm (1foot) apart in line with the wind. Light a fire between them. Use a shelf from your kitchen oven as a grill, resting it on the bricks. Replace the turf (and the grill!) after use.

5

It may sound obvious, but be sure to

find a hard, level, fireproof surface for your barbecue.

Many sites are not as stable as they appear. Turf, for example, looks solid enough, but the legs or wheels of a barbecue can sink alarmingly into it, especially when pushed down by an extra load of fuel or food.

6

When lighting a barbecue, use as few chemicals as possible.

Firelighters and lighter fuels are costly, and their smells can linger and taint the food. Much better to use scrunched up balls of newspaper covered with thin, dry kindling wood – dead twigs or split softwood (chopped-up shelving works a treat). Then add charcoal piece by piece.

7

Charcoal is the most popular type of barbecue fuel. It **burns very hot, and doesn't give off a lot of smoke.** And, of course, you can buy it in bags. Try to find charcoal which has been locally produced from sustainably managed woodland.

8

Add intriguing aromas to your cooking by burning other woods. Hardwoods such as apple, cherry, hazel and holly have especially lovely scents. So have prunings from grape vines and olive trees. Make sure all these materials are dry (not green) and cut into smallish chunks no thicker than your thumb.

9

Keep clear of wooden sheds and fences,

dead vegetation, thatched roofs and anything else combustible. Not only do barbecues get very hot – they can also send out showers of sparks which fly surprising distances and land in the most inconvenient places.

10

Heat Control Tip No.1:

juggling the coals. Wise control of heat is the secret of good, consistent barbecuing. The simplest method of increasing heat is to push the embers closer together and pile them up. To decrease heat, gently spread them apart again. Your technique will quickly improve with practice.

11

Heat Control Tip No.2:

adjust the grill height. It is wise to buy or build a barbecue which allows you to raise or lower your grill rack. This places it nearer or further from the heat, depending on whether you want to cook fast or slow. On home-made barbies, you can improvise with a couple of bricks on each side.

12

Heat Control Tip No.3:

fast food first. This is the simplest rule of all. Your fire should be at its hottest when you begin cooking. So first on the grill should go all steaks, burgers and food which requires fast searing. Later on, the temperature will drop. Now you can cook the food which needs slower and more delicate treatment.

13

Be patient.

Give the fire time to get going properly before you start cooking. It will take at least half an hour to create an even layer of smoke-free, glowing embers rather than roaring flames. Spraying on extra lighter fuel to speed things up is a catastrophically bad idea.

14

Keep your grill racks clean.

Do this on the spot – after cooking and before you pack everything away. **When** the grill has **cooled** down a bit, **rub off grease and gunk** with a damp cloth. Then scrape away the burnt-on bits with a good tough wire brush. This way, your grill will be reasonably clean when you next use it.

15

Heat up your grill racks before you start cooking.

As soon as the fire is lit, put the racks in place. They will soon get very hot, and leftover grease will quickly burn away. Give the bars another scrub with the wire brush.

16

Make sure you **have plenty of work surface space around the grill**

It's vital to have quick and easy access to plates, utensils and the dozens of other things a cook needs to hand. So surround yourself with tables, trolleys, wall tops and other heat resistant surfaces – the more the merrier.

17

Safety first.

Any fire is potentially dangerous. Keep a bucket of sand or a water hose (preferably connected) nearby just in case. You should also have a first aid box handy, to treat burns and other possible minor injuries.

18

There are

two essential cooking tools – a pair of tongs and a spatula.

Both should be of stainless steel and have good long handles sheathed in wood or another fire-resistant material. Buy the best you can afford. Badly-aligned tongs mean dropped food and frayed tempers.

19

Oil the grill rack before searing meat. This will

stop the meat from sticking to the metal.

Get yourself a long-handled brush (with natural, not nylon, bristles) or an old but clean cloth. When the grill is hot, anoint the mesh sparingly with groundnut or sunflower oil. Don't use olive oil – it burns more easily.

20

Wear oven gloves that are not just heatproof, but fireproof. Once again this may sound obvious, but barbecues get very hot. They can fire up utensils and racks to red heat on occasions. So look after your hands and forearms.

And wear a good sturdy **apron** to guard against fat splashes.

21

Hinged racks or baskets make a cook's life much easier. Clamp a delicate piece of **fish** between the two sides, and it **can be turned swiftly and** without damage. Hinged racks also **stop** skewered pieces of meat and other small morsels such as **vegetables from rolling** around or falling into the fire.

22

Scatter a few **woody herbs on the embers just before cooking.** Rosemary and juniper smoke adds an extra dimension to lamb. Try sage leaves for pork, bay and thyme for beef or chicken, and fennel stalks for fish. Use your imagination.

23

Put on plenty of fuel at the beginning.

Once the fire is going well, add a generous amount of fuel. This should produce enough glowing embers to barbecue everything you need. Resist the temptation to pile on more charcoal while food is cooking. It will immediately make the fire cooler and give out smutty smoke.

24

Marinades make most meat more marvellous.

Marinating serves two purposes: it adds flavour and it tenderizes the meat. There are scores of recipes for marinades to suit all needs, but choose carefully. Pay particular attention to the soaking times, which vary hugely.

25

Think before you marinate.

There are some meats which are quite tasty and tender enough on their own. A very fine fillet of beef, lamb or venison may even be over-dried by a strong marinade. Simply brush it with oil and lightly season just before cooking.

26

Get rid of excess fat.

Melted fat will fall in the fire, causing flare-ups and producing acrid smoke. Cut away as much outer fat as you can from meat before cooking. The same warning applies to oily marinades. Dab off excess marinating liquid, otherwise this too will drip onto the embers with smelly results.

27

Season the meat before grilling

– but not too long before. A sprinkling of pepper and salt will add crunch and savour to the taste.

But never put salt in a marinade. It will add to the drying effect of the vinegar or wine, drawing more moisture out of the meat and tending to toughen it.

28

A simple teriyaki marinade for beef kebabs.

Use good quality braising steak cut into chunks. Mix together equal quantities of soy sauce, sesame oil and rice wine or sherry vinegar. Add grated garlic, grated ginger root and a big pinch of sugar. Turn the beef chunks in the mixture, cover and leave in the refrigerator for 24 hours.

29

A simple herb marinade for lamb

chops or leg steaks. Into a glass bowl put the zest and juice of two lemons, and the juice of one orange. Mix in dried oregano (preferably Greek), two crushed garlic cloves and a generous grinding of black pepper. Coat the meat with this, cover and refrigerate for 24 hours.

30

A simple wine marinade for chicken joints.

Put equal quantities of oil (not olive) and white wine into a dish. Add grated onion and chopped garlic and – if it's fresh – some chopped French tarragon. Grate black pepper generously and mix. Buy some organic, corn-fed chicken joints, coat them in the marinade and refrigerate overnight.

31

In general,

treat pork and poultry gently.

Pork quickly dries up in a fierce searing heat. Chicken should be thoroughly cooked, never just blasted black on the outside to leave a raw red interior. **Grill** them both **slowly over a moderate heat,** and with regular basting.

32

Fish should only be marinated for a very short time.

No more than two hours in the refrigerator is quite enough for white fish and shellfish. Oily fish such as mackerel and sardine don't need marinating at all – just a brush of oil and a grind of salt and pepper before grilling.

33

A simple pastis and fennel **marinade for white fish and shellfish.** Lightly toast a tablespoon of fennel seeds and put them in a glass dish. Mix in the juice of one lemon, a glass of white wine, a slug of Pernod or another anise drink and a slug of oil. Coat the fish and refrigerate for one hour.

34

Get the best from pork chops and spare ribs by brushing them **with a barbecue glaze.**

This is a thick sauce which forms a protective outer layer on the meat and stops it drying out. It can also add an exciting taste. A good simple glaze can be mixed from crushed garlic, salt, brown sugar, French mustard, vinegar and a slug of rum.

35

Always give meat a rest after grilling.

Fierce heat causes meat to shed its juices, and a period of rest gives those juices a chance to soak back in. A steak or chop should be allowed five minutes on a warmed plate. Bigger pieces, such as a beef rib or butterflied leg of lamb, need at least fifteen minutes.

36

Mediterranean vegetables, such as peppers, aubergines and courgettes, **are perfect for barbecuing.** Cut them into big chunks, along with some red onions and blanched globe artichokes, and thread on metal skewers. Salt and leave for 30 minutes. Then season again and brush with oil before grilling for about 15 minutes, turning often.

37

Parboil sausages before you grill them. This has two advantages: it gets rid of some of the fat (which would otherwise drip into the fire), and ensures that they will be cooked on the inside. Cover with water and bring to the boil, simmering for about 5 minutes.

38

Grilled bruschetta (pronounced brus-ketta) is one of the easiest of all starters.

First, prepare a topping of peeled and chopped tomato, onion and red pepper, mixed with olive oil, basil and balsamic vinegar. Then toast slices of good Italian country bread on the grill.
Rub the surfaces with garlic, drizzle olive oil, and pop on the topping.

39

Aubergines, barbecued over wood, make a heavenly dip

Trim the ends and make a few slits in the skin. Then grill so that the skin scorches evenly (about 15 minutes). Scoop out the insides and whizz in a food processor with chopped onion and tomato, lemon juice, olive oil and dried oregano.

40

Remember –

a barbecue is more than just a grill. It is simply a source of heat like any other cooker, only more aromatic and dramatic. You can also cook with saucepans, frying pans, kettles and woks on top of the grill racks. Just be sure they have flameproof handles.

41

Skewer vegetables through their skins

rather than just through the flesh. The skins are much tougher and don't go soggy when cooked. This way the vegetables are much less likely to fall off into the coals.

42

Parboil before barbecuing small or **new potatoes**
whole **on skewers.**
Boil for five minutes, then drain and pat dry. Thread them onto the skewers alternately
with bay leaves and shallots
or chunks of onion.

43

Corn on the cob is the perfect barbecue vegetable. You only have to cook the outside, and they can be eaten with the fingers. Roll the cobs in melted butter mixed with crushed garlic, a couple of chopped chillies, salt and pepper. Then grill for about 10 minutes.

44

Bake potatoes or onions in the embers of the barbecue. Wrap them well in oiled pieces of aluminium foil and bury in the fire once it is past its fiercest. They will take between 20 and 30 minutes to cook through.

45

You can **grill** desserts too.

Core and slice some good firm dessert apples, and sprinkle with lemon juice and a mixture of sugar and ground cinnamon. When the fire has cooled to moderate, pop the slices on the grill for 4 minutes a side. Serve with toasted slices of brioche or sweet bread and a dollop of crème fraîche.

46

Bananas are the simplest of all fruits to cook. They come in their own natural wrapping, and the heat of baking transforms the insides to a lovely sugary mush. Give them about 7 minutes on the grill, turning regularly.

Slit the skins and serve **with a brandy butter enlivened with grated ginger root** or crushed cardamom seed.

47

Make your own fruit kebabs.

The choice is huge, but the tastiest should include chunks of pineapple, banana and pear, halved peaches or plums, or whole strawberries.

Use firm and slightly under-ripe fruit

thus less likely to fall off the skewers.
Grill for no more than 3 minutes.

48

A simple yoghurt sauce for dressing barbecued lamb or chicken.

Some grilled meat can be a little dry, and cries out for a sauce to dip in or dribble on. This one is a mixture of strained yoghurt, lemon juice, salt and crushed garlic. You can also add a teaspoon of smoked paprika, or finely chopped mint and cucumber.

49

A simple Korean dipping sauce for prawns and other **seafood.** In a blender, whizz together 4 parts good soy sauce, 1 part rice vinegar, 2 parts sesame oil, 1 small salad onion and a pinch of chilli powder. Add a big pinch of brown sugar at the end. Juggle with these ingredients to suit your own taste buds.

50

The simplest sauces of all are flavoured butters. They can be prepared a day or two ahead and refrigerated. Just soften the butter, mash in the flavouring and blob on the grilled food. Try chopped rosemary and chillies for lamb, dill for salmon, tarragon or basil for chicken, and chopped olives and sage for beef.

Andrew Langley

Andrew Langley is a knowledgeable food and drink writer. Among his formative influences he lists a season picking grapes in Bordeaux, several years of raising sheep and chickens in Wiltshire and two decades drinking his grandmother's tea. He has written books on a number of Scottish and Irish whisky distilleries and is the editor of the highly regarded anthology of the writings of the legendary Victorian chef Alexis Soyer.

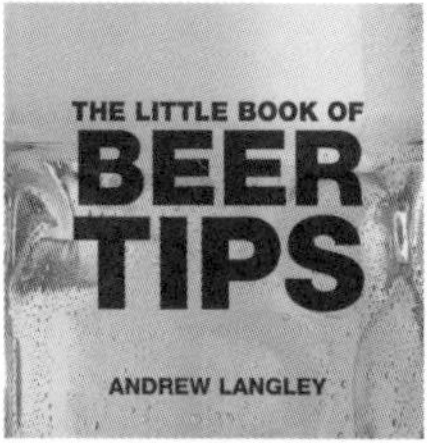

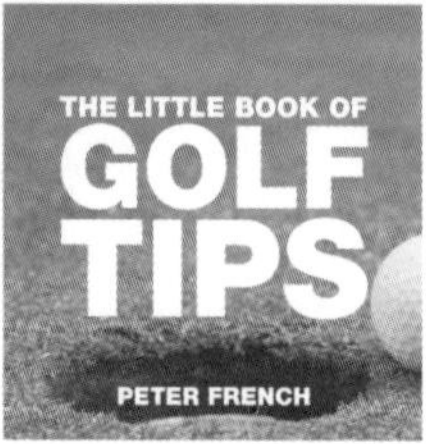

THE LITTLE BOOK OF

TIPS SERIES

THE LITTLE BOOK OF
CHEESE
TIPS
ANDREW LANGLEY

THE LITTLE BOOK OF
WINE
TIPS
ANDREW LANGLEY

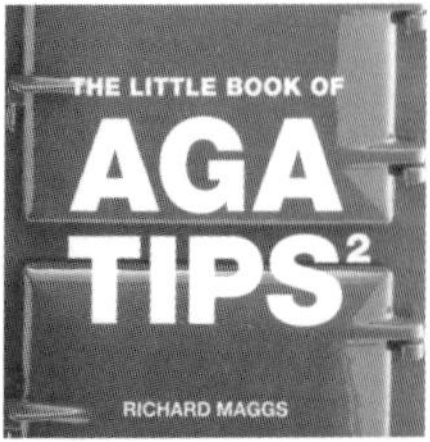
THE LITTLE BOOK OF
AGA
TIPS 2
RICHARD MAGGS

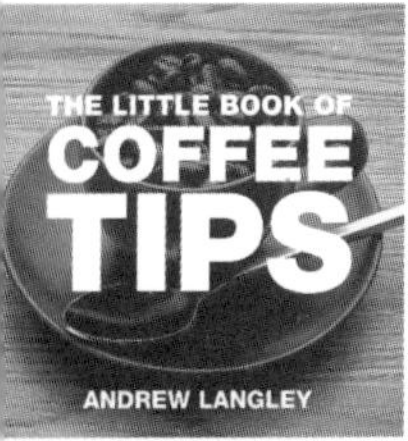
THE LITTLE BOOK OF
COFFEE
TIPS
ANDREW LANGLEY

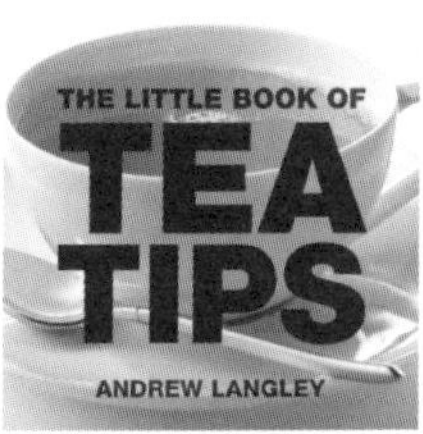
THE LITTLE BOOK OF
TEA
TIPS
ANDREW LANGLEY

THE LITTLE BOOK OF
AGA
TIPS 3
RICHARD MAGGS

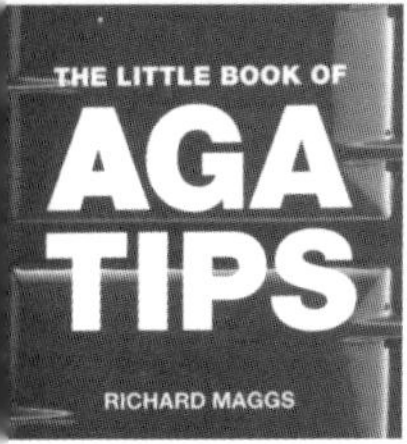
THE LITTLE BOOK OF
AGA
TIPS
RICHARD MAGGS

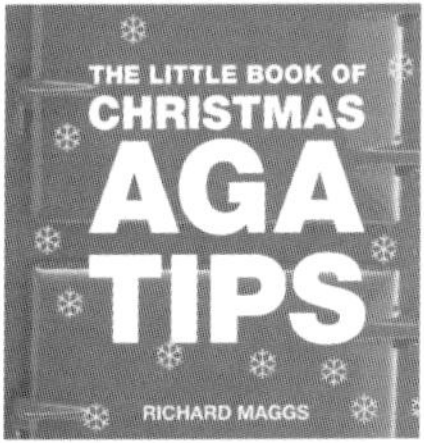
THE LITTLE BOOK OF
CHRISTMAS
AGA
TIPS
RICHARD MAGGS

THE LITTLE BOOK OF
RAYBURN
TIPS
RICHARD MAGGS

THE LITTLE BOOK OF
BRIDGE
TIPS
PETER FRENCH

THE LITTLE BOOK OF
CHESS
TIPS
PETER FRENCH

THE LITTLE BOOK OF
FISHING
TIPS
MICK DEVENISH

THE LITTLE BOOK OF
GREEN
TIPS
WILLIAM FORTT

THE LITTLE BOOK OF
KITTEN
TIPS
ANDREW LANGLEY

MARMITE
PAUL HARTLEY
THE LITTLE BOOK OF
MARMITE
TIPS

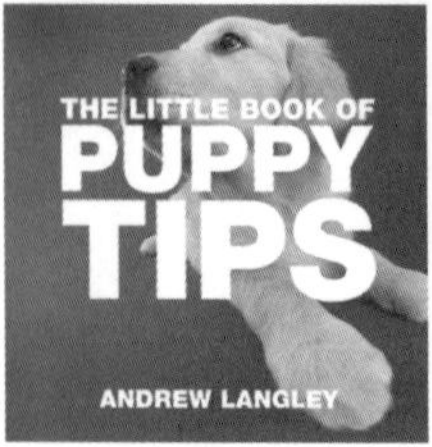
THE LITTLE BOOK OF
PUPPY
TIPS
ANDREW LANGLEY

THE LITTLE BOOK OF
WHISKY
TIPS
ANDREW LANGLEY

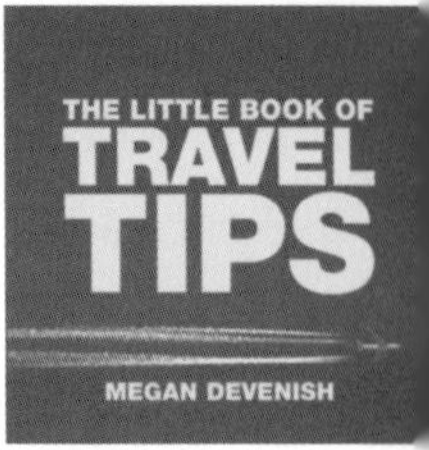
THE LITTLE BOOK OF
TRAVEL
TIPS
MEGAN DEVENISH